THE RESOURCE FOR
SMALL GROUP WORSHIP

THE RESOURCE FOR SMALL GROUP WORSHIP

VOLUME THREE

Devised by
Chris Bowater

Kevin Mayhew

First published in 2000 by
KEVIN MAYHEW LTD
Buxhall
Stowmarket
Suffolk IP14 3BW

ISBN 1 84003 512 9
ISMN M 57004 669 0
Catalogue No. 1450172

Illustrations by E. Margaret Inkpen
Cover design by Jonathan Stroulger
Edited by Helen Elliot
Project Co-ordinator: Asher Gregory

Printed in Great Britain

Important Copyright Information Regarding the Songs in this Book

The Publishers wish to express their gratitude to the copyright owners who have granted permission to include copyright material in this book. Details are indicated on the respective pages and on the acknowledgements page.

The **words** of the songs in this publication are covered by a **Church Copyright Licence** which allows local church reproduction on overhead projector acetates, in service bulletins, songsheets, audio/visual recording and other formats.

The **music** in this book is covered by the 'add-on' **Music Reproduction Licence** issued by CCL (Europe) Ltd and you may photocopy the music and words of the songs in this book provided:

- You hold a current Music Reproduction Licence from CCL (Europe) Ltd.
- The copyright owner of the hymn or song you intend to photocopy is included in the Authorised Catalogue List which comes with your Music Reproduction Licence.

Full details of both the Church Copyright Licence and the additional Music Reproduction Licence are available from:

Christian Copyright Licensing (Europe) Ltd
PO Box 1339
Eastbourne
East Sussex
BN21 1AD

Tel: 01323 417711
Fax: 01323 417722
e-mail: info@ccli.co.uk
WEB: www.ccli.com

Please note, all texts and music in this book are protected by copyright and if you do *not* possess a licence from CCL (Europe) Ltd, they may *not* be reproduced in any way for sale or private use without the consent of the copyright owner.

Creative Team

Devised by Chris Bowater

Editorial	E. Margaret Inkpen & Carol Woodcock
Writers	Jane Amey, E. Margaret Inkpen, Jo Pimlott, Pat Turner
Illustrations	E. Margaret Inkpen
Audio	Laurie Blackler & Daniel Bowater

Recorded at dB Studios, Lincoln

The Resource for Small Group Worship has been devised with convenience, variety and flexibility in mind. Taking into account also the breadth of worship experience and expression, this resource seeks to provide creative opportunities for 'all-age worship' without being either too condescending or too academic.

Contents

How to Use
The Resource for Small Group Worship

Convenience For the all-too-busy group leader, this resource provides a complete worship experience that includes:

- Worship songs: gently contemporary, easy to follow without being predictable.
- Meditation: wordless worship, a time to pause, reflect, consider and listen to God.
- Bible readings: arranged for corporate, responsive or personal reading.
- Prayers: written in non-religious language, for corporate or personal use.
- Discussion topics: touching issues of faith, essentials of life, challenges in society.
- Creative activities: always fun, never too exclusive, certain to build group relationships.

Each worship session comes in two parts:

1 The Notes for Leader preparation section, which comprises:

  – an introduction to the theme
  – a list of resources required
  – notes for leading the session, with extracts from
  – relevant books and materials for further activities.

2 Worship Session material. The following icons are used to identify each section of the worship material or format. *Only pages with a large underlying icon may be photocopied, or pages of artwork to be used by the group:*

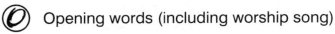

(O) Opening words (including worship song)

(M) Meditation and listening to God

(R) Reading from the Bible

(P) Prayer and praise (including worship songs)

Further activities, discussion, study and creative ideas

 Closing words

A full programme would take about 1 hour to complete.

Variety In order to provide as wide a range of material as possible, each volume of *The Resource for Small Group Worship* contains:

- three sessions of general worship
- one session aimed at families and children
- one session which focuses on social awareness and specific issues.

Flexibility *The Resource for Small Group Worship* can be used more selectively by leaders looking for:

- song selection
- meditation ideas
- thematic material
- specialist topics – e.g. social awareness, church festivals, seasonal issues, special occasions
- group activities – drama, craft-work and suchlike
- written prayers.

Though much of the groundwork has been done here for the group leader, the role of that leader is still crucial. Enlist the help of the Holy Spirit at all times so that the worship is truly 'in Spirit and truth'. Lead the people into an experience that more than fills a programme but also affects their homes, marriages, relationships, attitudes, and jobs: their whole lives.

May this resource be a blessing to you, your groups and churches.

Chris Bowater

SESSION 11

Notes for Leader

Session 11: General Worship

THEME: HOLY SPIRIT

Introduction to theme

Approaching the subject of the Holy Spirit in this time of worship and study is to expect that he will make his presence known within your group. However this does not mean that issues such as speaking in tongues, prophesying, healing, etc. need to be raised. The Holy Spirit will move in God's own time and in his way. The worship will still be directed towards God, who sent his Holy Spirit. We can communicate with God, through the Spirit, because God is Spirit. Each person may experience the presence of the Spirit in a different way and may need to express this during the meeting.

The purpose of the session is to explore and discover the function of the Holy Spirit and the different ways in which he related to people in the Bible.

Resources required

You will need enough copies of the session for your group.

Worship songs:

These will be found on Album 3, tracks 1-4.

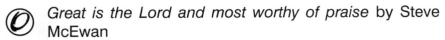 *Great is the Lord and most worthy of praise* by Steve McEwan

Holy Spirit, we welcome you by Chris Bowater

 *I receive your love* by Paul Armstrong

Meditation track – *Pastorale*

Copies of the list of references for study and discussion.

Preparation

 Meditation and listening to God

Read the following extract from *One in the Spirit* by David Watson, published by Hodder & Stoughton, 1973:

> Love more than anything else is the hallmark of the Spirit's presence. The fruit of the Spirit is love. The love of God is poured into our hearts by the Holy Spirit. The coming of the Holy Spirit at Pentecost meant that the apostles were enveloped by the love of God and it was this love that was their compelling, motivating power.
>
> It is interesting to note that on five occasions in Acts we read that the Spirit 'fell' on people. In four other passages in the New Testament, that same word 'fell', is used in the context of an affectionate embrace. The father of the prodigal son 'fell on his neck and kissed him' – could this suggest that the 'falling' of the Holy Spirit on his people is like a divine embrace, a wonderful holy hug?
>
> A sure sign of the Holy Spirit's activity in our lives is a deep, personal love relationship with Jesus. 'God's love has been poured into our hearts through the Holy Spirit which has been given to us' (Romans 5:5).

Suggested time for meditation: 3-5 minutes.

Before moving on, allow time for the group to share any thoughts arising from the time of meditation.

Further activity

Introduction to theme

Leader We will be looking at when, how and for what purpose the Holy Spirit was manifested throughout the Bible. As the third member of the Trinity, God's Spirit has an integral part to play in our lives, so it is important to know what this purpose is.

From passages in Romans, Corinthians, Galatians, Ephesians, John's Epistle and Thessalonians, we can discover many aspects of the Holy Spirit's impact on our lives. He gives an assurance that we are set free, that we can know what God desires, that we have life and peace, that we are children of God, that we are helped in weakness.

I know that the Spirit intercedes for me, guides me, gives me words, is the truth; that the Spirit lives in me, that I have eternal life, that I am sealed for redemption. I can pray in the Spirit, know the power of the Spirit, bear the fruit of the Spirit, take up the sword of the Spirit, and discern the truth about God and Jesus Christ.

The following references can be distributed to members of the group to read, or the pages of references can be cut up for small groups to match the verses to the references/ headings. Continue with discussion.

Material for study and discussion

Genesis 1:2. The Spirit took part in creation.

Now the earth was formless and empty, darkness was over the surface of the deep and the Spirit of God was hovering over the waters.

Genesis 6:3. The Spirit 'contended' with man.

Then the Lord said, 'My Spirit will not contend with man for ever, for he is mortal.'

Exodus 31:1-5. The Spirit is given for skill, ability and knowledge; in artistic gifting.

The Lord said to Moses . . . 'I have filled Bezalel with the Spirit of God, with skill, ability and knowledge in all kinds of crafts – to make artistic designs.'

Numbers 11:25. The Spirit revealed the power of God to a small group (in prophecy).

Then the Lord came down in the cloud and spoke with Moses, and he took the Spirit that was on him and put the Spirit on the seventy elders. When the Spirit rested on them, they prophesied.

Judges 6:34; 11:29. The Spirit gives leadership power.

Then the Spirit of the Lord came upon Gideon and he blew the trumpet to summon tribes to follow him.

Then the Spirit of the Lord came upon Jephthah . . . and he advanced against the Ammonites and the Lord gave them into his hands.

1 Samuel 16:13. The Spirit comes with anointing for leadership.

Samuel took the horn of oil and anointed David in the presence of his brothers and from that day on, the Spirit of the Lord came upon David in power.

Nehemiah 9:30. The Spirit teaches, guides and disciplines.

For many years you were patient with your people. By your Spirit you admonished them through your prophets.

Isaiah 61:1. The Spirit gives strength for specific tasks.

The Spirit of the sovereign Lord is on me, because the Lord has anointed me to preach good news to the poor.

Matthew 1:18b, 20b. The Holy Spirit took a major role in Jesus' conception.

Mary was found to be with child through the Holy Spirit.

Joseph, son of David, do not be afraid to take Mary home as your wife, because what is conceived in her is from the Holy Spirit.

Matthew 3:16. The Spirit prepared Jesus for ministry.

As soon as Jesus was baptised, he went up out of the water. At that moment heaven was opened, and he saw the Spirit of God descending like a dove and lighting on him.

Matthew 10:19-20. The Spirit speaks through people.

Do not worry about what to say or how to say it. At that time you will be given what to say, for it will not be you speaking, but the Spirit of your Father speaking through you.

John 14:26. The Spirit teaches and reminds us of Jesus' words.

The Counsellor, the Holy Spirit, whom the Father will send in my name, will teach you all things and will remind you of everything I have said to you.

John 16:13. The Spirit guides us in truth.

When the Spirit of truth comes, he will guide you into all truth.

Acts 1:8. The Spirit gives power for witnessing around the world.

You will receive power when the Holy Spirit comes on you; and you will be my witnesses . . . to the ends of the earth.

Acts 2:4, 6, 11. The Spirit enabled the apostles to speak in foreign languages.

They were filled with the Holy Spirit and began to speak in other tongues as the Spirit enabled them . . . A crowd came together in bewilderment because each person heard them speaking in his own language. They said, 'We heard them declaring the wonders of God in our own tongue.'

Acts 4:31. The Spirit gives us power to speak boldly.

They were all filled with the Holy Spirit and spoke the word of God boldly.

List of extra references used in Leader's introduction:

Romans 8:2, 5, 6, 14, 26-27; 5:5

1 Corinthians 2:4, 10, 11, 13; 6:19

Galatians 5:22-23; 6:8

Ephesians 4:30; 6:17-18

1 Thessalonians 5:19

1 John 4:2, 6

Revelation 2:7

Worship Session 11

THEME: HOLY SPIRIT

Opening words

Leader The words spoken by the prophet Joel: God says, 'In the last days I will pour out my Spirit on all people. Your sons and daughters will prophesy and your young men will see visions, your old men will dream dreams.' (Acts 2:16)

Group *God is Spirit and his worshippers must worship him in Spirit and in truth.*
(John 4:24)

Leader Do you not know that your body is a temple of the Holy Spirit who is in you, whom you have received from God? You are not your own, you were bought at a price.
(1 Corinthians 6:19)

Group *Those who live in accordance with the Spirit have their minds set on what the Spirit desires.*
(Romans 8:5)

Worship song

Great is the Lord and most worthy of praise
Steve McEwan

Great is the Lord and most worthy of praise,
the city of our God, the holy place,
the joy of the whole earth.

Great is the Lord, in whom we have the victory.
He aids us against the enemy,
we bow down on our knees.

And, Lord, we want to lift your name on high,
and, Lord, we want to thank you
for the works you've done in our lives;
and, Lord, we trust in your unfailing love,
for you alone are God eternal,
throughout earth and heaven above.

Reading from the Psalms

Leader O Lord, hear my prayer;
listen to my cry for mercy;
in your faithfulness and righteousness
come to my relief.

Group *Do not bring your servant into judgement*
for no one living is righteous before you.

Leader My spirit grows faint within me;
my heart within me is dismayed.

Group *I remember the days of long ago,*
I meditate on all your works
and consider what you have done.

Leader I spread out my hands to you;
my soul thirsts for you like a parched land.

Group *Answer me quickly, O Lord;*
my spirit faints with longing.
Do not hide your face from me,
or I will be like those who go down into the pit.

Leader Let the morning bring me word of your unfailing love,
for I have put my trust in you.
Show me the way I should go,
for to you I lift up my soul.

Group *Rescue me from my enemies, O Lord,*
for I hide myself in you.
Teach me to do your will,
for you are my God;
may your Holy Spirit lead me on level ground.

Leader For your name's sake, O Lord, preserve my life. (Psalm 143, omitting verses 3 and 12)

To close

Group *Those who live in accordance with the Spirit have their minds set on what the Spirit desires.*

Meditation and listening to God

The thought for meditation is taken from *One in the Spirit* by David Watson.

To close

Leader God is Spirit and his worshippers must worship him in Spirit and truth.

Prayer and praise

Leader Let us concentrate our thoughts on the work of the Holy Spirit as we talk to God in thanksgiving and praise.

Members of the group can use the following short individual prayers:

'Create in me a clean heart, O God
and renew a steadfast spirit within me.'
Thank you for the Holy Spirit's presence in my life, Lord.
Keep me steadfast in my walk with you.

Amen.

Paul says: 'My message and preaching were not with persuasive words but with a demonstration of the Spirit's power.'
Lord, thank you for the power of your Spirit working in us.

Amen.

'The Spirit helps us in our weakness.'
Father we all have times of weakness.
Send your Holy Spirit to help us
and give us strength.

Amen.

'Our bodies are temples of the Holy Spirit.'
Lord, help us to honour you with our bodies
and not grieve the Holy Spirit
by what we do in our lives.

Amen.

I pray, O God, that you will see
the fruit of the Holy Spirit
evident in us . . . 'love, joy, peace,
patience, kindness, goodness, faithfulness,
gentleness and self control'.

Amen.

Father, keep the fire of your Holy Spirit
burning within us.
Renew us with excitement
and a desire to see the power of your Spirit
working in us.

Amen.

'He who has an ear, let him hear
what the Spirit is saying to the churches.'
Lord, we want to listen to the voice of the Holy Spirit.
Help us to understand and accept
what you have to say.

Amen.

Leader Father, thank you that we have a Spirit
who intercedes on our behalf.
Thank you for sending your Spirit
to comfort, counsel and guide us.
Thank you that as we pray together,
your Holy Spirit is with us,
putting into words the things we cannot say.

(Short pause)

Amen.

Worship songs

Holy Spirit, we welcome you
Chris Bowater

Holy Spirit, we welcome you.

Holy Spirit, we welcome you.

Move among us with holy fire,

as we lay aside all earthly desires,

hands reach out, and our hearts aspire.

Holy Spirit, Holy Spirit,

Holy Spirit, we welcome you.

Holy Spirit, we welcome you.

Holy Spirit, we welcome you.

Let the breeze of your presence blow,

that your children here might truly know

how to move in the Spirit's flow.

Holy Spirit, Holy Spirit,

Holy Spirit, we welcome you.

Holy Spirit, we welcome you.

Holy Spirit, we welcome you.

Please accomplish in me today

some new work of loving grace, I pray;

unreservedly have your way.

Holy Spirit, Holy Spirit,

Holy Spirit, we welcome you.

I receive your love
Paul Armstrong

I receive your love,

I receive your love,

in my heart I receive your love, O Lord.

I receive your love

by your Spirit within me,

I receive, I receive your love.

I confess your love,

I confess your love,

from my heart I confess your love, O Lord.

I confess your love

by your Spirit within me,

I confess, I confess your love.

(Spontaneous worship and prayer may continue.)

Further activity

Introduction to theme

Leader We will be looking at when, how and for what purpose the Holy Spirit was manifested throughout the Bible. As the third member of the Trinity, God's Spirit has an integral part to play in our lives, so it is important to know what this purpose is.

From passages in Romans, Corinthians, Galatians, Ephesians, John's Epistle and Thessalonians, we can discover many aspects of the Holy Spirit's impact on our lives. He gives an assurance that we are set free, that we can know what God desires, that we have life and peace, that we are children of God, that we are helped in weakness.

I know that the Spirit intercedes for me, guides me, gives me words, is the truth; that the Spirit lives in me, that I have eternal life, that I am sealed for redemption. I can pray in the Spirit, know the power of the Spirit, bear the fruit of the Spirit, take up the sword of the Spirit, and discern the truth about God and Jesus Christ.

Closing words

Leader God is Spirit and his worshippers must worship him in Spirit and in truth.

Group *Holy Spirit, we welcome you.*

All Amen.

Great is the Lord and most worthy of praise

Words and Music: Steve McEwan

Holy Spirit, we welcome you

Words and Music: Chris Bowater

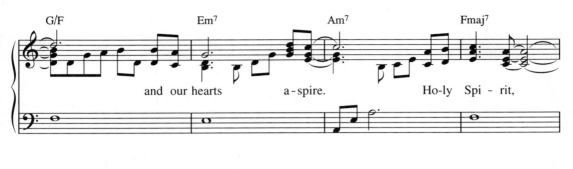

and our hearts a-spire. Ho-ly Spi - rit,

Ho-ly Spi - rit, Ho-ly Spi - rit,

To next verse

we wel-come you.

Last time

you.

2. Holy Spirit, we welcome you.
Holy Spirit, we welcome you.
Let the breeze of your presence blow,
that your children here might truly know
how to move in the Spirit's flow.
Holy Spirit, Holy Spirit,
Holy Spirit, we welcome you.

3. Holy Spirit, we welcome you.
Holy Spirit, we welcome you.
Please accomplish in me today
some new work of loving grace, I pray;
unreservedly have your way.
Holy Spirit, Holy Spirit,
Holy Spirit, we welcome you.

/us
/we

I receive your love

Words and Music: Paul Armstrong

2. I confess your love,
   I confess your love,
   from my heart I confess your love, O Lord.
   I confess your love
   by your Spirit within me,
   I confess, I confess your love.

SESSION 12

Notes for Leader

Session 12: General Worship

THEME: JOY

Introduction to theme

The aim of this worship session is to look into the subject of joy from a Biblical viewpoint. Bear in mind that not every person in the group will be full of joy at the time of the meeting. Some may be suffering pain or sickness; some may be grieving or worried; others angry, resentful or stressed. Whatever our situations, we can still explore 'the joy of the Lord' and its impact on our praise and worship. When our focus is on the Lord, we can make a 'choice to rejoice'.

The purpose of the session is to explore and discover the function of the Holy Spirit and the different ways in which he related to people in the Bible.

Resources required

You will need enough copies of the session for your group.

Worship songs:

These will be found on album 3, tracks 5-8.

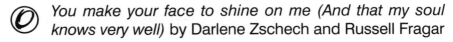 *You make your face to shine on me (And that my soul knows very well)* by Darlene Zschech and Russell Fragar

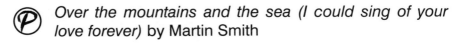 *Over the mountains and the sea (I could sing of your love forever)* by Martin Smith

You make my heart feel glad by Patricia Morgan and Sue Rinaldi

 Meditation track – *Take a break*

For the study and discussion:

- overhead or large sheet of paper
- sheets printed with headings (see page 41)
- slips of paper with references (see page 42)
- glue sticks.

 If you choose to use the creative activity, you will need:

- copies of the JOY verse (see page 45)
- felt pens, crayons and stickers
- construction paper (various colours)
- glue sticks.

Preparation

 Meditation and listening to God

Quote from *The Hallelujah Factor* by Jack Taylor, published by Highland Books, 1985.

Introduction to meditation

In his book *The Hallelujah Factor* Jack Taylor reminds us that we have a 'choice to rejoice'! It is not easy to find joy in all situations and circumstances, but our joy is *in the Lord*.

- It worked for Nehemiah: 'Do not grieve, for the joy of the Lord is your strength.'

- It worked for David: 'God turned my wailing into dancing; He removed my sackcloth and clothed me with joy.'

- It worked in Paul's prison cell: 'Rejoice in the Lord always and again I say rejoice!'

- It worked for Habakkuk: 'Though the fig tree does not have buds and there are no grapes on the vine; though the olive crop fails and the fields produce no food; though there are no sheep in the field and no cattle in the stalls, yet I will rejoice in the Lord! I will be joyful in God my Saviour. The Sovereign Lord is my strength.'

Extract from *Each New Day* by Corrie Ten Boom, published by Spire Books, Fleming H. Revell Company, (a division of Baker Book House) Grand Rapids, Michigan, USA.

Corrie Ten Boom tells a story about a parachutist.

'How did you feel when you jumped out of the aeroplane with your parachute for the first time?' she asked. He answered, 'I only had one thought: It works! It works!'

In her experience of concentration camps, Corrie found joy in her Lord and Saviour, Jesus. She says of that: 'It works! It works!'

Suggested time for meditation: 3-5 minutes.

Before moving on, allow time for the group to share any thoughts arising from the time of meditation.

Further activity

Material for study and discussion:

Notes to leader for creative ways of using the material:

either

a) your group could divide into pairs or threes, each group having a copy of the list of 'headings' on the next page, which can be photocopied. The small groups also need glue and an envelope containing the 17 verse references printed on individual pieces of paper (see page 42 for photocopying). Give plenty of time for the groups to look up the references and decide under which heading each should be glued. The leader can use the notes included below to develop a discussion on the subject.

or

b) the list of 'headings' can be printed on an overhead for projection, or on a large sheet of paper. References can be given to individuals, who read the verses to the group. Everyone decides under which heading the leader should include the reference. The notes given under each heading below can be used to summarise.

Leader's introduction to the subject:

Joy is a spontaneous response to God, his creation of the world around us and his work in our lives. It wells up from the heart and bursts out – in shouting, singing, laughing, clapping, and dancing, as we can see in the Bible.

The word joy is used 240 times in the New International Version of the Bible; rejoice or rejoicing, 50 times; gladness, 100 times; sorrow or sadness are referred to 8 times.

God's message of salvation, his kingdom and his love are good reasons for expressing joy!

Headings

GOD'S JOY

JESUS' JOY

HOLY SPIRIT JOY

HEAVENLY JOY

JOY OF GOD'S PEOPLE

MESSAGE OF JOY

JOY IN NATURE

References to Joy

ROMANS 15:13

JOHN 17:13

1 THESSALONIANS 1:4-6

JOB 38:4, 6-7

LUKE 15:4-7

EZRA 3:11-13

NEHEMIAH 8:5, 9-10

LUKE 24:51-53

ACTS 8:6-8

ACTS 16:34

1 PETER 1:8-9

JAMES 1:2-3

LUKE 2:10-11

PSALM 65:12-13

ISAIAH 44:23

ISAIAH 55:12

LUKE 19:38-40

Notes for Leader

GOD'S JOY   ROMANS 15:13

Leader's comment:

God wants to fill us with joy so that we overflow with hope.

JESUS' JOY   JOHN 17:13

Leader's comment:

We need to read the words of Jesus in the Gospels for a full measure of joy.

HOLY SPIRIT JOY   1 THESSALONIANS 1:4-6

Leader's comment:

In accepting the Gospel and the power of the Holy Spirit, the believers experienced a deep sense of joy in spite of suffering. The Thessalonians became a model to others and their faith became known everywhere.

HEAVENLY JOY   JOB 38:4, 6-7

Leader's comment:

On at least two occasions we find joy among the angels in heaven, at creation and when sinners come to repentance. Does our response to these important events reflect this joy?

JOY OF GOD'S PEOPLE	EZRA 3:11-13
	NEHEMIAH 8:5, 9-10
	LUKE 24:51-53
	ACTS 8:6-8
	ACTS 16:34
	1 PETER 1:8-9
	JAMES 1:2-3

Leader's comment:

These verses show evidence of people filled with joy. What made them so happy? (Ask the readers of each verse for answers)

MESSAGE OF JOY	LUKE 2:10-11

JOY IN NATURE	PSALM 65:12-13
	ISAIAH 44:23
	ISAIAH 55:12
	LUKE 19:38-40

NEHEMIAH 8:10

Cut out verse along dotted line, colour, decorate with stickers, and glue to a sheet of A4 construction paper. Keep as a visual reminder!

Worship Session 12

THEME: JOY

Opening words

Leader Jesus said, 'If you obey my commands, you will remain in my love, just as I have obeyed my Father's commands and remain in his love. I have told you this so that my joy may be in you and your joy may be complete.'
(John 15:10-11)

Group *The joy of the Lord is my strength.*
(Nehemiah 8:10)

Leader Praise be to the God and Father of our Lord Jesus Christ! In his great mercy he has given us new birth into a living hope through the resurrection of Jesus Christ from the dead, and into an inheritance that can never perish, spoil or fade, kept in heaven for you. Even though you have not seen Jesus . . . you believe in him and are filled with an inexpressible and glorious joy, for you are receiving the goal of your faith, the salvation of your souls.
(1 Peter 1:3-4, 8-9)

Group *The joy of the Lord is my strength.*

Worship song

**You make your face to shine on me
(And that my soul knows very well)**
Darlene Zschech and Russell Fragar

You make your face to shine on me,

and that my soul knows very well.

You lift me up, I'm cleansed and free,

and that my soul knows very well.

When mountains fall I'll stand

by the power of your hand

and in your heart of hearts I'll dwell,

and that my soul knows very well.

Joy and strength each day I find,

and that my soul knows very well.

Forgiveness, hope, I know is mine,

and that my soul knows very well.

Reading from the Psalms

Leader Keep me safe, O God,
for in you I take refuge.

Group *I said to the Lord, 'You are my Lord;*
apart from you I have no good thing.'

Leader Lord, you have assigned me my portion and my cup;
you have made my lot secure.

Group *The boundary lines have fallen for me in pleasant*
places; surely I have a delightful inheritance.

Leader I will praise the Lord who counsels me;
even at night my heart instructs me.

Group *I have set the Lord always before me.*
Because he is at my right hand,
I shall not be shaken.

Leader Therefore my heart is glad and my tongue rejoices;
my body also will rest secure,
because you will not abandon me to the grave,
nor will you let your Holy One see decay.

Group *You have made known to me the path of life,*
you will fill me with joy in your presence,
with eternal pleasures at your right hand.

Leader Praise be to the God and Father of our Lord Jesus Christ!

Group *The joy of the Lord is my strength.*
(From Psalm 16)

Meditation and listening to God

Thought for meditation

Leader In his book *The Hallelujah Factor* Jack Taylor reminds us that we have a 'choice to rejoice'! It is not easy to find joy in all situations and circumstances, but our joy is in the Lord.

Corrie Ten Boom tells a story about a parachutist.

'How did you feel when you jumped out of the aeroplane with your parachute for the first time?' she asked. He answered, 'I only had one thought: It works! It works!'

In her experience of concentration camps, Corrie found joy in her Lord and Saviour, Jesus. She says of that: 'It works! It works!'

To close

Leader I will be joyful in God, my Saviour. The Sovereign Lord is my strength. He makes my feet like the feet of a deer. He enables me to go up to the high places.
(Habakkuk 3:19)

Prayer and praise

Worship songs

Over the mountains and the sea
(I could sing of your love forever)
Martin Smith

Over the mountains and the sea
your river runs with love for me,
and I will open up my heart
and let the Healer set me free.
I'm happy to be in the truth,
and I will daily lift my hands,
for I will always sing of
when your love came down.

I could sing of your love for ever,
I could sing of your love for ever,
I could sing of your love for ever,
I could sing of your love for ever.

O, I feel like dancing,
it's foolishness, I know;
but when the world has seen the light,
they will dance with joy
like we're dancing now.

You make my heart feel glad
Patricia Morgan and Sue Rinaldi

You make my heart feel glad,
you make my heart feel glad;
Jesus, you bring me joy,
you make my heart feel glad.

Lord, your love brings healing
and a peace into my heart;
I want to give myself in praise to you.
Though I've been through heartache,
you have understood my tears:
O Lord, I will give thanks to you.

When I look around me
and I see the life you made,
all creation shouts aloud in praise;
I realise your greatness –
how majestic is your name!
O Lord, I love you more each day.

© 1990 Kingsway's Thankyou Music

Prayers

Members of the group read out each verse, followed by a spontaneous prayer of thanksgiving and praise. (The leader should make it clear that the spontaneous prayers are optional.)

Psalm 118:24

This is the day the Lord has made;
let us rejoice and be glad in it.

Amen.

Psalm 126:3

The Lord has done great things for us,
and we are filled with joy.

Amen.

Psalm 16:11

You have made known to me the path of life;
you fill me with joy in your presence,
with eternal pleasures at your right hand.

Amen.

Psalm 5:11

Let all who take refuge in you be glad
let them ever sing for joy.

Amen.

Psalm 31:7

I will be glad and rejoice in your love
for you saw my afflictions
and knew the anguish of my soul.

Amen.

Psalm 71:23

My lips will shout for joy when I sing praises to you –
I, whom you have redeemed.

Amen.

Psalm 92:4

For you make me glad by your deeds, O Lord;
I sing for joy at the work of your hands.

Amen.

Isaiah 12:3

With joy you will draw water from the wells of salvation.

Amen.

Isaiah 51:11

The ransomed of the Lord will return . . . with singing
and everlasting joy will crown their heads;
gladness and joy will overtake them
and sorrow and sighing will flee away.

Amen.

Isaiah 61:10

My soul rejoices in my God.
For he has clothed me with garments of salvation
and arrayed me in a robe of righteousness.

Amen.

The group may want to continue in praise, or repeat
the worship songs.

To close

Leader   I will be joyful in God, my Saviour.
He enables me to go up to high places.

Group   *The joy of the Lord is my strength.*

Further activity

Material for study and discussion

Joy is a spontaneous response to God, his creation of
the world around us and his work in our lives. It wells
up from the heart and bursts out – in shouting, singing,
laughing, clapping, and dancing, as we can see in the
Bible.

The word joy is used 240 times in the New International
Version of the Bible; rejoice or rejoicing, 50 times; gladness, 100 times; sorrow or sadness are referred to 8
times.

God's message of salvation, his kingdom and his love
are good reasons for expressing joy!

Closing words

Leader So be joyful always, pray continually; give thanks in all circumstances, for this is God's will for you in Christ Jesus.
(1 Thessalonians 5:16-18)

Group *I will be joyful in God, because he enables me to go up to high places with the feet of a deer.*
Amen.

You make your face to shine on me
And that my soul knows very well

Words and Music: Darlene Zschech and Russell Fragar

2. Joy and strength each day I find,
   and that my soul knows very well.
   Forgiveness, hope, I know is mine,
   and that my soul knows very well.

Over the mountains and the sea
I could sing of your love for ever

Words and Music: Martin Smith

O-ver the moun-tains and the sea your ri-ver runs with love for me,

and I will o - pen up my heart and let the Heal - er set me free.

I'm hap-py to be in the truth, and I will dai - ly lift my hands,

for I will al - ways sing of when your love came down.

I could sing of your love for e - ver, I could sing of your love

You make my heart feel glad

Words and Music: Patricia Morgan and Sue Rinaldi

With a steady rock rhythm

2. When I look around me
   and I see the life you made,
   all creation shouts aloud in praise;
   I realise your greatness –
   how majestic is your name!
   O Lord, I love you more each day.

SESSION 13

SESSION 10

Notes for Leader

THEME: HEALING

Introduction to theme

The subject of healing, how to pray for healing, who receives it, why and in what situations, whether physical, spiritual or mental, cannot be addressed in this short session, which is primarily for worship. Healing can, however, occur during worship and each of us needs a touch from the hand of God. Keep the focus on God, and on his Son who died for us, accepting the love, forgiveness and healing which they offer and remaining confident that one day there will be no more pain, no more suffering, and no tears.

Resources required

You will need enough copies of the session for your group.

Worship songs:

These will be found on Album 3, tracks 9-12.

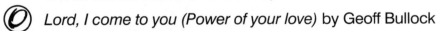 *Lord, I come to you (Power of your love)* by Geoff Bullock

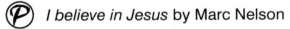 *I believe in Jesus* by Marc Nelson

Be still and know (Unknown)

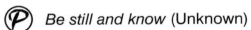 Meditation track – *Melody of the waves*

For study and discussion:

- paper and pens.

For the creative activity:

- coloured card
- pictures of scenes from travel brochures
- glue and scissors
- pens
- Bibles.

Preparation

 Meditation and listening to God

Read the following extract from *Sea Edge* by W. Phillip Keller, published by Word (UK) Ltd.

Everywhere, in a hundred ways, the ocean waters heal. The seashore has an atmosphere of serenity, beauty, strength and invigoration that stimulates the whole of man. It is more, much more, than merely a balm for the body. The sea can restore weary minds, strained emotions, flagging wills, and aching hearts. It possesses healing properties.

Often, as I stroll along the shore, or sit quietly contemplating the grandeur of the deeps, the Spirit of God reminds me that similarly he is my great healer. It is he that restores my soul. It is he that renews my spirit. It is he who imparts to my life the health and the wholesomeness of his own character.

I deliberately surrender my will to his will. I allow God's love to sweep over me as the waves on the seashore wash the sand clean. The daily impact of his life on mine brings vigour and vitality. It ensures health and holiness and wellbeing.

Suggested time for meditation: 3-5 minutes.

Before moving on, allow time for the group to share any thoughts arising from the time of meditation.

Prayer and praise

How the group feels about participating in a physical act of prayer does not really matter, as everyone will have their eyes closed, so participation is optional. But it is quite amazing how just the small act of using one's hands to express worship can open doors. Encourage your group to try it!

 Further activity: study and discussion

The following suggestions are in note form with questions and subjects to encourage discussion. The references used describe some of Jesus' healing miracles and show how he understood the needs of the people. In each situation his attitude and words were different. It is suggested that small groups study one of the miracles each, and bring their answers back to the larger group for general discussion. They will need copies of pages 68 and 69, pens and paper.

As an introduction to the discussion, look at the words of Jesus from the Sermon on the Mount, which appear in Matthew chapters 5-7, before the healing miracles, which are recorded in chapters 8 and 9.

The Sermon on the Mount

- Our needs are known by the Father before we ask.

- We need not be anxious about our lives.

- We should seek first the kingdom and God's righteousness.

- We need to accept the promise that everyone who asks, receives.

Miracles of healing

Group A
Matthew 8:2-3: Jesus heals a leper

1 Discuss the situation – a leper wants to reach Jesus through a large crowd.

2 Write down what the leper did and said.
What does it tell you about how he felt?

3 What did Jesus do? Remember, it was against the law to touch a leper.
What does it tell us about Jesus?

4 Jesus' words: 'I am willing.'
Discuss other times he said this, e.g. in the garden of Gethsemane.
'Be clean.' Discuss this response to the specific need of the leper.

Group B
Matthew 8:5-13: Jesus heals the centurion's servant

1 Discuss the relative positions of a centurion and a servant.
What can we learn about their relationship?

2 Consider the position of a centurion asking Jesus, an itinerant Jewish preacher, for help.
What can we learn about the centurion from his words?

3 How does Jesus respond? What was Jesus' reaction to the centurion?

4 How does the healing take place?

5 What can we learn from this account about faith?

Group C
Matthew 8:14-15: Jesus heals Peter's mother-in-law

1 Friends and families were important to Jesus, not just strangers and big crowds.
How do we react to illness in our own homes?

2 What did Jesus do and say?
Make a list of the positives which result from the touch of someone who cares.

3 What happened after Peter's mother-in-law was healed?
What does 'serving Jesus' mean? (Look up Matthew 25:35-36, 40.)

Group D

Matthew 9:2-7: Jesus heals the paralysed man

1 Discuss where the healing took place – how might this affect people?

2 What can we learn about friends; about being in it all together;
  about agreeing a plan of action?

3 Look at Jesus' words. Divide the sentence up into phrases and write down
  the significance of each word.
  Which is the most important part for you?

4 What did the man have to do? (v.6) Compare with Matthew 8:22.
  Jesus sends us into different situations.

5 What was the reaction of those who witnessed what happened?

Group E

Matthew 9:20-22: Jesus heals an unknown woman

1 What was the situation when the woman approached Jesus?

2 What can we learn about the woman – what was she like?

3 What can we learn about healing from Jesus' words, 'Who touched me?'
  Is this relevant for those involved in the healing ministry today?

4 How would you feel if you were the woman in this situation?
  Write down what you imagine her feelings to be, before, during and after
  the event.

Group F

Matthew 9:18-19, 23-25: Jesus heals the ruler's daughter

1 What can we find out about the ruler from his words and reactions?
  What does he want?

2 What did Jesus do? Make a list, from the moment the ruler approache
  him to when he left the house.

3 Look at this event from the point of view of:
  • the child's mother   • a disciple
  • the doctor treating the child   • the daughter herself

Optional creative activity

Making cards for those who need a special word or blessing.

Using a piece of coloured card (stationery or art suppliers have a wide variety, with envelopes to match), choose pictures from travel brochures (you can dream of holiday locations and sunshine!) – lakes, mountains, sunsets with palm trees, waterfalls – to glue on the card, with a verse of encouragement. Psalms, Isaiah and the Gospels provide a wonderful selection.

Worship Session 13

THEME: HEALING

Opening words

Leader Cast your cares on the Lord and he will sustain you, he will never let the righteous fall.
(Psalm 55:22)

Group *Surely God is my help;*
the Lord is the one who sustains me.
(Psalm 54:4)

Leader He took up our infirmities and carried our sorrows.
He was pierced for our transgressions.
He was crushed for our iniquities.
By his wounds we are healed.
The Lord has laid on him the iniquity of us all.
(From Isaiah 53)

Group *Surely God is my help,*
the Lord is the one who sustains me.

Leader A man with leprosy came and knelt before Jesus, saying, 'Lord, if you are willing, you can make me clean.' Jesus reached out his hand and touched the man. 'I am willing,' he said. 'Be clean.'

Group *Lord, I come to you. Reach out your hand and touch me.*
You can make me clean.

Worship song

Lord, I come to you
(Power of your love)
Geoff Bullock

Lord, I come to you,
let my heart be changed, renewed,
flowing from the grace
that I found in you.
And, Lord, I've come to know
the weaknesses I see in me
will be stripped away
by the power of your love.

Hold me close,
let your love surround me,
bring me near,
draw me to your side;
and as I wait,
I'll rise up like an eagle,
and I will soar with you;
your Spirit leads me on
in the power of your love.

Lord, unveil my eyes,
let me see you face to face,
the knowledge of your love
as you live in me.
Lord, renew my mind
as your will unfolds in my life,
in living every day
in the power of your love.

Reading from the Psalms

Leader He who dwells in the shelter of the Most High
will rest in the shadow of the Almighty.

Group *I will say of the Lord, 'He is my refuge and my fortress,*
my God in whom I trust.'

Leader He will cover you with his feathers
and under his wings you will find refuge;
his faithfulness will be your shield and rampart.

Group *We will not fear the terror of the night,*
nor the danger that comes by day,
nor the illness that stalks in the darkness,
nor the disease that destroys at midday.

Leader If you make the Most High your dwelling –
even the Lord, who is my refuge –
then no harm will befall you,
no disaster will come near your home.

Group *He will command his angels concerning us,*
to guard us in all our ways;
they will lift us up in their hands,
so that we will not strike a foot against a stone.

Leader 'Because he loves me,' says the Lord, 'I will rescue him,
I will protect him, for he acknowledges my name.
He will call upon me and I will answer him;
I will be with him in trouble,
I will deliver him and honour him.
With long life I will satisfy him
and show him my salvation.'

(Adapted from Psalm 91)

Group *My soul finds rest in God alone,
my salvation comes from him.
He alone is my rock and my salvation;
he is my fortress, I shall never be shaken.*

Leader Find rest, O my soul, in God alone;
my hope comes from him.
My salvation and honour depend on God;
he is my mighty rock, my refuge.

Group *Trust in him at all times; pour out your hearts to him,
for God is our refuge.*

(Adapted from Psalm 62)

Leader Cast your cares on the Lord and he will sustain you.

Group *Surely God is my help;
the Lord is the one who sustains me.*

Meditation and listening to God

The thought for meditation is based on a reading from *Sea Edge* by W. Phillip Keller.

To close

Leader Wash over me, Lord.
Make me clean; make me whole.
I surrender my will to your will.

Prayer and praise

How you feel about participating in a physical act of prayer does not really matter, as everyone will have their eyes closed, so participation is optional. But it is quite amazing how just the small act of using one's hands to express worship can open doors. Try it!

Leader In this time of talking with God, we will do something a bit different. With our eyes closed, let us open our hands in a gesture of openness to God and acceptance of all that he is offering.

Group member *Our hands are open to you, Lord. We don't want to hold anything back. Touch us with your healing power; pour out your saving grace. You carry my sorrows, you heal me by your own wounds; your death and resurrection have given me life. With open hands I receive you now.*

(Pause)

Leader Let us now turn our hands over, face down. Clench them into tight fists . . . and now relax them.

Group member *Lord, you say we can cast our cares on to you, and you will sustain us. My hands are open to show that I have let go of my burdens, and my worries – the things that weigh me down, and seem to control my life. You have borne our sins and carried our sorrows. Nothing is too difficult for you. I will trust in your love, Lord.*

(Pause)

Leader Now we stretch out our hands in front as if we are reaching out to touch something, or laying our hands on someone.

Group member *Jesus, we stretch out our hands, hands which have received you and laid down their burdens. We reach out, not for ourselves, but for those who are on our hearts who need a special touch from you. We bring them to you now. You know their situations, Lord; bless them, and heal them.*

(Individuals can name people who they know need healing.)

(Pause)

Leader Let us hold hands together.

Group member *Through hand touching hand, we express our oneness in Jesus Christ; we share friendship, caring for each other, encouraging each other. We give one another strength and comfort. We pray for safety. None of us needs feel alone. Let us spend a moment praying for the people on our right and left.*

(Pause)

Leader Jesus said these words to those he healed: 'Take heart . . . be encouraged . . . go in peace . . . by faith you are made whole . . . get up and walk.'

Let's say the words of the grace to each other:

All May the grace of our Lord Jesus Christ,
and the love of God
and the fellowship of the Holy Spirit
be with us now and for evermore. Amen.

Worship songs

I believe in Jesus
Marc Nelson

I believe in Jesus;

I believe he is the Son of God.

I believe he died and rose again,

I believe he paid for us all.

And I believe he's here now

(I believe that he's here),

standing in our midst.

Here with the power to heal now

(with the power to heal),

and the grace to forgive.

I believe in you, Lord;

I believe you are the Son of God.

I believe you died and rose again,

I believe you paid for us all.

And I believe you're here now

(I believe that you're here),

standing in our midst.

Here with the power to heal now

(with the power to heal),

and the grace to forgive.

Be still and know
Unknown

Be still and know that I am God,
be still and know that I am God,
be still and know that I am God.

I am the Lord that healeth thee,
I am the Lord that healeth thee,
I am the Lord that healeth thee.

In thee, O Lord, do I put my trust,
in thee, O Lord, do I put my trust,
in thee, O Lord, do I put my trust.

A time of prayer for special needs may follow.

Further activity

Material for study and discussion

The references we are going to look at describe some of Jesus' healing miracles and show how he understood the needs of the people. In each situation his attitude and words were different.

Closing words

Leader If Jesus touched peoples' lives then – he can touch ours now. His words – 'be clean', 'take heart', 'such faith', 'get up' – are for us, too. We can go to find him, kneel before him, touch him, acknowledge his power and authority, and serve him. It is through Jesus that we find healing.

Lord, I come to you
Power of your love

Words and Music: Geoff Bullock

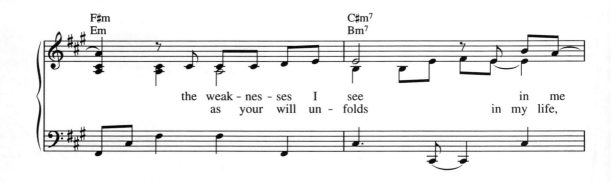

the weak - nes - ses I see in me
as your will un - folds in my life,

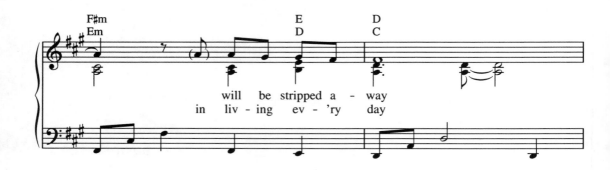

will be stripped a - way
in liv - ing ev - 'ry day

by the pow'r of your love.
in the pow'r of your love.

Chorus

Hold me close, let your love sur - round

I believe in Jesus

Words and Music: Marc Nelson

With conviction

I
I be-lieve in Je - sus;
I be-lieve in you, Lord;

I be-lieve he is the Son of God.
I be-lieve you are the Son of God.

I be-lieve he died and rose a-gain,
I be-lieve you died and rose a-gain,

I be - lieve he paid for us all.
I be - lieve you paid for us all.

Be still and know

Words and Music: Unknown

2. I am the Lord that healeth thee . . .

3. In thee, O Lord, do I put my trust . . .

SESSION 14

Notes for Leader

Session 14: Family Worship (all-age)

THEME: CREATION

Introduction to theme

This can be a session with lots of activity and visual aids!

The purpose is to praise and worship our Creator God and explore the wonders of nature. Children and adults can be involved throughout, with the verbal responses, reading of the Psalm and spontaneous prayers. Using picture cut-outs for the Psalm and actions for the song will involve even the younger children. Slides (if available) could be used to illustrate the short prayer written by Jane Amey. Look through the additional creative activity ideas to find ones appropriate for your meeting.

When we wake up to the qualities of the God who created this amazing world in which we live, 'we are without excuse' (Romans 1:20) – praise will come naturally.

Resources required

You will need enough copies of the session for your group.

Worship songs:

These will be found on Album 3, tracks 13-16.

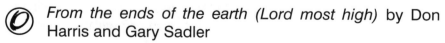 *From the ends of the earth (Lord most high)* by Don Harris and Gary Sadler

 *Big, mighty and strong* by Tom Beardmore

 *All things bright and beautiful* by Cecil Frances Alexander

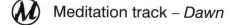 Meditation track – *Dawn*

Depending on your choice of activity, you will need:

- sheets of A4 paper
- coloured pens, pencils, crayons
- small cards with Bible verses, facts and pictures
- posters/pictures of the 7 'days' of creation
- large cards with the numbers 1-7
- pictures from calendars, travel brochures, garden or outdoor magazines, catalogues etc.
- glue sticks
- a long piece of newsprint or wallpaper
- thick black felt pen.

If you decide to illustrate your session with slides, you will need a projector, screen and appropriate transparencies.

This would be an ideal opportunity to hang banners or posters depicting scenes of natural wonders to provide visual aids.

Preparation

 Meditation and listening to God

Introduce the meditation with this Scripture:

For since the creation of the world, God's invisible qualities – his eternal power and divine nature – have been clearly seen, being understood from what has been made, so that men are without excuse (Romans 1:20).

Ask someone to read the poem *If* by Jo Pimlott.

Suggested time for meditation: 2 minutes. Before moving on, allow time for the group to share any thoughts arising from the time of meditation.

(F) Further activity

Material for study and discussion:

Repeat the verse from Romans 1:20:

Leader For since the creation of the world, God's invisible qualities – his eternal power and divine nature – have been clearly seen, being understood from what has been made, so that men are without excuse.

These are some amazing facts about God's creation of our natural world. (Pictures or overhead projection can be used as illustrations.)

Mountains

All 10 of the world's highest mountains are in the Himalayas. No one can agree on the exact heights of the tallest mountains - people have never been able to make a machine accurate enough to measure them exactly!

Your righteousness is like the mighty mountains,
your justice like the great deep.
O Lord, you preserve both man and beast.
How priceless is your unfailing love!
Both high and low among men find refuge
in the shadow of your wings.
(Psalm 36:6-7)

Seas

Over 70 per cent of the earth's surface is covered by sea. It is estimated that there are about 7 million tons of salt in every cubic mile of seawater!

The seas have lifted up, O Lord,
the seas have lifted up their voice;
the seas have lifted up their pounding waves.
Mightier than the thunder of the great waters,
mightier than the breakers of the sea –
the Lord on high is mighty.
(Psalm 93:3-4)

Stars

There are at least 100,000 million stars in the Milky Way.
Our nearest star neighbour is 25 million miles away!

When I consider your heavens,
the work of your fingers,
the moon and the stars,
which you have set in place,
what is man that you are mindful of him,
the son of man that you care for him?
(Psalm 8:3-4)

Ants

Ants are amazing creatures. They work efficiently together, wage war and even capture slaves. They have an excellent sense of direction and can be frozen for long periods without harm. Ants and termites have been known to burrow to a depth of nearly 24 metres in search of water.

Go to the ant, you sluggard;
consider its ways and be wise!
It has no commander,
no overseer or ruler,
yet it stores its provisions in summer
and gathers its food at harvest.
(Proverbs 6:6-8)

Trees

The General Sherman Giant Sequoia is thought to be the biggest tree in the world. It is 31.3 metres in circumference, nearly 84 metres tall and has enough wood in it to make 5 billion matches. It is the largest living object on the planet.

You will go out in joy
and be led forth in peace;
the mountains and hills
will burst into song before you,
and all the trees of the field
will clap their hands.
(Isaiah 55:12)

 Activity for all ages

Turn this into an all-age activity by giving everyone in the group a card with either the fact, the Bible verse, or a picture on it (enlarge and photocopy pages 94-95). The pictures could be given to the younger children. By moving around the room and talking to each other, people sort themselves into appropriate small groups. They can then, in turn, read the Bible verses to the whole gathering.

All Age Activity

Enlarge and photocopy these two pages.

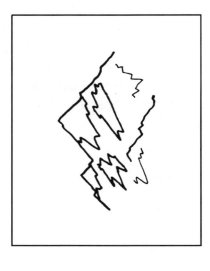

PSALM 36:6-7:

Your righteousness is like the mighty mountains, your justice like the great deep. O Lord, you preserve both man and beast. How priceless is your unfailing love! Both high and low among men find refuge in the shadow of your wings.

PSALM 93:3-4:

The seas have lifted up, O Lord, the seas have lifted up their voice; the seas have lifted up their pounding waves. Mightier than the thunder of the great waters, mightier than the breakers of the sea – the Lord on high is mighty.

FACT:

All 10 of the world's highest mountains are in the Himalayas. No one can agree on the exact heights of the tallest mountains – people have never been able to make a machine accurate enough to measure them exactly!

FACT:

Over 70 per cent of the earth's surface is covered by sea. It is estimated that there are about 7 million tons of salt in every cubic mile of seawater.

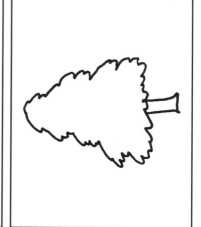

PSALM 8:3-4:

When I consider your heavens, the work of your fingers, the moon and the stars, which you have set in place, what is man that you are mindful of him, the son of man that you care for him?

PROVERBS 6:6-8:

Go to the ant, you sluggard; consider its ways and be wise! It has no commander, no overseer or ruler, yet it stores its provisions in summer and gathers its food at harvest.

ISAIAH 55:12:

You will go out in joy and be led forth in peace; the mountains and the hills will burst into song before you, and all the trees of the field will clap their hands.

FACT:

There are at least 100,000 million stars in the Milky Way. Our nearest star neighbour is 25 million miles away!

FACT:

Ants and termites have been known to burrow to a depth of nearly 24 metres in search of water. An ant can carry many times its own body weight.

FACT:

The General Sherman Giant Sequoia is thought to be the biggest tree in the world. It is 31.3 metres in circumference, nearly 84 metres tall and has enough wood in it to make 5 billion matches. It is the largest living object on the planet.

Additional material for creative activities

Order out of chaos

You will need:

- large pictures or posters depicting scenes of creation, i.e. light and dark, sky, land, sea, plants, sun, moon, stars, a calendar, fish, birds, animals, humans, one blank
- large cards with the numbers 1-7.

Purpose: to learn the order of creation, during the seven Biblical days.

How to use this activity:

- Ask 7 young people to stand at the front holding each of the numbered cards in order 1–7.
- Give pictures to children (or adults).
- Leader asks the group to call out which day is correct for individual pictures in turn. The child holding the picture then stands in front of the chosen number.
- The group can change its mind and move children from one number to another, eventually bringing 'order out of chaos'!
- There will be more children with pictures in front of certain numbers, but each day will have at least one picture.

Everyone can share in creation

a) you will need:

- A4 paper
- crayons
- pencils and pens.

Purpose: to draw a picture of something one enjoys in nature (a flower, mountain, sea, animal, and bird etc.)

These pictures can then be used during the prayer and praise time to thank God for his creation.

b) you will need:
- a large sheet of paper for a mural
- glue sticks
- pictures from magazines, catalogues etc. of natural wonders or scenes.

Purpose: to create a mural of natural wonders of our world.

Seeing is believing

Visualise the Psalm used during the worship (Psalm 148).

You will need:
- cut out pictures for the verses i.e. angel, sun, moon, star, cloud, rain, whale, ocean (depths), lightning, snow, mountain, apple tree, lion, mouse, cow and bird.

Purpose: to encourage young children to take part in the reading by giving them a special part to play.

How to use this activity:

Children or adults are given the picture cut-outs before reading the Psalm. When the appropriate word is spoken in the Psalm, the child with the picture can go to the front of the group, or hold up their picture.

Solve the clues

Choose a verse about the creation theme (see example on the following page) and present it to the group on a long piece of newsprint or wallpaper. You don't need to be a brilliant artist to make simple clues!

You will need:

- a long piece of paper
- a thick black felt pen.

Purpose: to solve the clues and learn a Bible verse.

How to use this activity:

Ask for two young people (or adults – children may be too small to hold the paper up high) to hold each end of the paper so it can be seen by the group, or pin it to a wall. Ask the group (especially children) to solve each word in turn and read the completed verse with reference.

Solve the Clues Example

Psalm 150:6

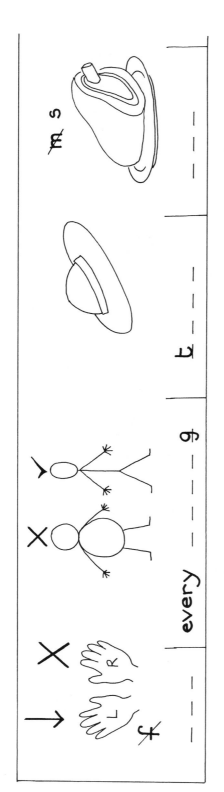

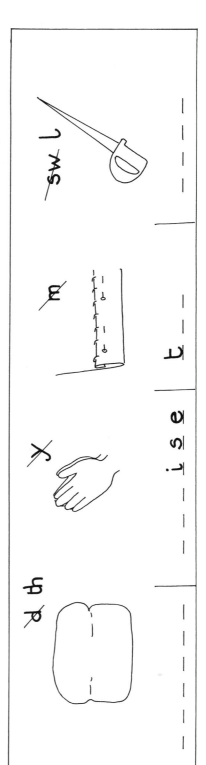

Worship Session 14

THEME: CREATION

Opening words

Leader O Lord, our Lord, how majestic is your name in all the earth!
(Psalm 8:1)

Group *You made everything and everything belongs to you.*

Worship song

From the ends of the earth
(Lord most high)
Don Harris and Gary Sadler

From the ends of the earth
(from the ends of the earth),
from the depths of the sea
(from the depths of the sea),
from the heights of the heavens
(from the heights of the heavens),
your name be praised;

from the hearts of the weak
(from the hearts of the weak),
from the shouts of the strong
(from the shouts of the strong),
from the lips of people
(from the lips of people),
this song we raise, Lord.

Throughout the endless ages
you will be crowned with praises,
Lord most high;
exalted in every nation,
Sovereign of all creation,
Lord most high, be magnified.

Reading from the Psalms

Leader   Let everything that has breath praise the Lord.
(Psalm 150:6)

Group   *Praise the Lord from the heavens,*
praise him in the heights above.

Leader   Praise him, all his angels,
praise him, all his heavenly hosts.

Group   *Praise him, sun and moon,*
praise him, all you shining stars.

Leader   Praise him, you highest heavens
and you waters above the skies.

Group   *Let them praise the name of the Lord,*
for he commanded and they were created.

Leader   He set them in place for ever and ever;
he gave a decree that will never pass away.

Group   *Praise the Lord from the earth,*
you great sea creatures and all ocean depths,
lightning and hail, snow and clouds,
stormy winds that do his bidding;

Leader   You mountains and all hills,
fruit trees and all cedars,
wild animals and all cattle,
small creatures and flying birds;

Group   *Kings of the earth and all nations,*
you princes and all rulers on earth,
young men and maidens, old men and children.

Leader Let them praise the name of the Lord,
for his name alone is exalted;
his splendour is above the earth and the heavens.

Group *He has raised up for his people a horn,*
the praise of all his saints,
of Israel, the people close to his heart.

All Praise the Lord.
(Psalm 148)

To close

Leader O Lord, our Lord, how majestic is your name in all the earth.

Group *You made everything and everything belongs to you.*

Meditation and listening to God

Thought for meditation:

For since the creation of the world, God's invisible qualities – his eternal power and divine nature – have been clearly seen, being understood from what has been made, so that men are without excuse.

(Romans 1:20)

Poem: *If* by Jo Pimlott

If I could paint,
I would paint you seas of green and endless blue,
and birds and trees and flowers too.
I would seek to catch the shafts of light,
the colour of the velvet night
dotted with stars. And I would try

to copy the colours of a sunset sky;
to somehow capture every shape and shade,
your glory, which is shown through all you've made,
if I could paint.

If I could write,
I would find words to say how much you care
for your world and the people who live there;
and I would seek to somehow share that love
and set out plain the truth of it and prove
that God was man and walked here as we do,
and all that Jesus said and did was true.
And I would hope my words would somehow bring
more honour and more glory to my king,
if I could write.
If I could sing,
I'd find the kind of songs that lift the soul;
not opera or folk or rock and roll,
but somehow in a style all of my own
I'd sing and share the joy that I have known.
My heart would lift and I would feel so free
to let the music soar and just be me.
And like the shouting birds I'd play my part
and pray my songs would reach and touch your heart,
if I could sing.

Creator God,
I cannot paint or even write or sing;
I cannot bring to you what others bring.
And though I know so often I compare
the things I have with gifts that others share,
I know you give creative gifts and skill
for every one of us to use at will.
And all I have I offer up to you
that your life might be seen in all I do,
Creator God.

Prayer and praise

Leader Let us pray to our God, the creator of all things.
Sovereign Lord, your glory abounds in every area of
creation.

Group *We praise you.*

Leader From the tiniest form to the vast beauty of the landscape,
your greatness is made known.

Group *We praise you.*

Leader The awesome magnificence of the mountain's
rocky crags
and great depths of the ocean
cry out your majesty.

Group *We praise you.*

Leader In the whisper of the breeze,
and each detail of the leaves,
the goodness of our God is declared.

Group *We praise you,*
we praise you,
we praise you.

All Amen.

Allow time for spontaneous prayers, thanking and
praising God.

Worship songs

Big, mighty and strong
Tom Beardmore

My God, is big, he's mighty,
he's powerful and strong,
my God, is big, he's mighty and strong.
My God, is big, he's mighty,
he's powerful and strong,
my God, is big, mighty and strong.

I love you, Jesus, I know you love me,
I want to bow before you,
bow down on my knees.
I want to bow down every day,
stay here where I belong.
I wanna be your willing servant
'cos you're big, you're mighty and strong.

We're all so very diff'rent,
with diff'rent coloured skin,
some people are tall and fat
and some are small and thin.
One day we'll be together,
one day before too long,
we'll all bow down before you,
'cos you're big, you're mighty and strong.

All things bright and beautiful

Cecil Frances Alexander

All things bright and beautiful,
all creatures great and small,
all things wise and wonderful,
the Lord God made them all.

Each little flower that opens,
each little bird that sings,
he made their glowing colours,
he made their tiny wings.

The purple-headed mountain,
the river running by,
the sunset and the morning
that brightens up the sky.

The cold wind in the winter,
the pleasant summer sun,
the ripe fruits in the garden,
he made them every one.

He gave us eyes to see them,
and lips that we may tell
how great is God Almighty,
who has made all things well.

Further activity

Material for study and discussion

For since the creation of the world, God's invisible qualities – his eternal power and divine nature – have been
clearly seen, being understood from what has been
made, so that men are without excuse.
(Romans 1:20)

Closing words

Leader The heavens declare the glory of God;
the skies proclaim the work of his hands.
Day after day they pour forth speech;
night after night they display knowledge.
There is no speech or language where their
voice is not heard.
Their voice goes out into all the earth,
their words to the ends of the world.

In the heavens he has pitched a tent for the sun,
which is like a bridegroom
coming forth from his pavilion,
like a champion rejoicing to run his course.
It rises at one end of the heavens
and makes its circuit to the other;
nothing is hidden from its heat.
(Psalm 19:1-6)

Leader O Lord, our Lord, how majestic is your name in all the
earth.

Group *You made everything and everything belongs to you.*

All Amen.

From the ends of the earth
Lord most high

Words and Music: Don Harris and Gary Sadler

Big, mighty and strong

Words and Music: Tom Beardmore

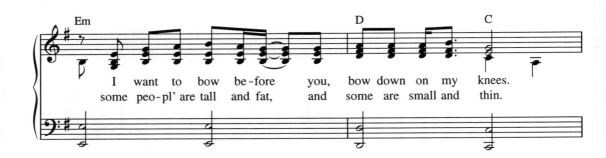

I want to bow be-fore you, bow down on my knees.
some peo-pl' are tall and fat, and some are small and thin.

I want to bow down ev - 'ry day, stay here where I be - long.
One day we'll be to - ge-ther, one day be - fore too long,

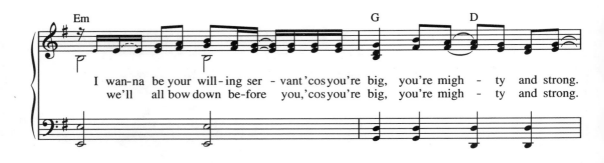

I wan-na be your will-ing ser - vant 'cos you're big, you're migh - ty and strong.
we'll all bow down be-fore you, 'cos you're big, you're migh - ty and strong.

My God is

All things bright and beautiful

Words: Cecil Frances Alexander
Music: Traditional English Melody

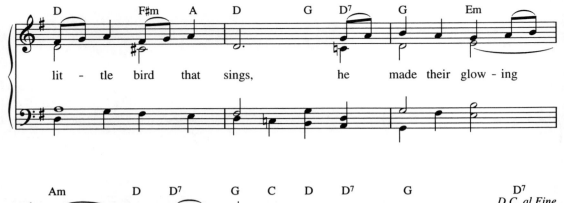

lit - tle   bird   that   sings,   he   made   their   glow - ing

D.C. al Fine

co - lours,   he   made   their   ti - ny   wings.

2. The purple-headed mountain,
   the river running by,
   the sunset and the morning
   that brightens up the sky.

3. The cold wind in the winter,
   the pleasant summer sun,
   the ripe fruits in the garden,
   he made them ev'ry one.

4. He gave us eyes to see them,
   and lips that we may tell
   how great is God Almighty,
   who has made all things well.

SESSION 15

Notes for Leader

Session 15: Social Awareness, Specific Issues

THEME: GLOBAL PERSPECTIVE

Introduction to theme

Some people may be called by God to work overseas, some are involved in projects to help developing countries, some are 'prayer warriors', but many of us still have only a limited knowledge of countries mentioned every day in the media, and know even less about the people God created to inhabit the earth.

The worship in this section is directed to a great and mighty God who has a global perspective and plan, which involves us. Travel is getting easier, people visit remote places for a holiday; churches are being planted, thousands of people are coming to know Jesus; God is at work. But do we know what he is doing?

You might consider inviting others in your community who are from different ethnic backgrounds to an open meeting, in order to help break down barriers, widen horizons, confront ignorance, suspicion and misconceptions. Do we take Mark 16:15 seriously?

Resources required

You will need enough copies of the session for your group.

Worship songs:

These will be found on Album 3, tracks 17-20.

 We want to see Jesus lifted high by Doug Horley

 We shall stand by Graham Kendrick

Lord, have mercy (Prayer song) by Graham Kendrick

 Meditation track – *Floating*

 A globe or open world atlas as a visual aid.

 Letters, articles from overseas countries.

(F) **Further activity**

Activity 1

- copies of world map, see page 125
- newspaper articles, holiday brochure pictures, etc
- pens and pencils.

Activity 2

- copies of list of countries/places, see page 126
- paper
- pens and pencils
- optional, copies of world map, see page 125.

Activity 3

- large cardboard box
- pictures of places around the world (from travel brochures)
- glue.

Activity 4

- copies of list of Bible travellers, see page 127
- pencils and pens.

Activity 5

- 3 copies of drama script *Jonah, the Reluctant Evangelist*, by Pat Turner.

Preparation

 Meditation and prayer

Use a globe or map as a focus for meditation as you read through the following:

Leader 'From heaven the Lord looks down and sees all mankind.'

In this time of meditation try to work your way around the world from country to country, visualising the different areas and the people who inhabit them.

Think of the frozen regions of the Arctic, with days when the sun never rises, and the temperature plunges to 50 degrees below freezing. Think of the Inuit people.

Think of the scorching deserts of North Africa, with nomadic people moving from one waterhole to another.

Think of the crowded cities of India and the East, with rich and poor, Muslim, Hindu and Buddhist – a different way of life.

Think of the green cultivated landscape of New Zealand with more sheep than people, snow-capped mountains and brilliant flowers.

Think of the great mountain ranges of the Himalayas, the Andes, the Rockies – the people who live at altitudes higher than Britain's highest mountain.

Think *big* - think of the world. There are 8 billion people living in the world today. Think of the world.

Suggested time for meditation: 3-5 minutes. Before moving on, allow time for the group to share any thoughts arising from the time of meditation.

Prayer and praise

You may have specific mission projects in other countries and people whom you support – this is the time to read letters about their work, get up-dates on their prayer needs and find out more about their situations. Individuals in your group may have friends or relatives working overseas who can show glimpses of their lives and their countries. Prepare your group beforehand so they can bring pictures, letters etc. with them. Write the prayer needs and countries on a large sheet of paper.

There may be situations around the world which need to be remembered in prayer. Praise God for any breakthrough or event which is positive. Use weekly or daily newspapers to remind the group of the 'world in action'.

Remember that we are part of this world. Pray for opportunities to make an impact on the world – sometimes just a letter (or an e-mail), a donation or sponsorship, can help; but God can use the prayers of faithful people in mighty ways, too. You might even consider supporting someone in a short-term mission capacity or even send a member of your group!

 Further activity

The emphasis in this session is on developing a global perspective. The group might continue to look at a variety of issues including other religious viewpoints, the positive and similar aspects of world religions, and the group's fears or suspicions, ignorance or misconceptions.

If there are people in the community from other ethnic backgrounds, you could organise an informal meeting and invite them to speak to your group, seeking to break down barriers and show genuine interest and care; especially if they are new to the area and have problems with culture or language.

Activity 1

Divide the group into twos or threes with copies of the world map (page 125), a sheet of newspaper articles, numbered pictures from travel brochures, etc. and a pen/pencil. Allow 10-15 minutes to identify each country on the map. (For instance, a picture of the ancient Borobodur temples would be located in Indonesia!)

Activity 2

Give small groups the name of a country or island (they could pick the names from a box, using the countries listed on page 126). Ask each group to write down all they know about the country – its people, economics, history, geography, religion, etc. (It may be surprising how little we find we know about the rest of the world!) Using the map (page 125) they could write the name of the country in its location in the world.

Activity 3

Using a large cardboard box (or strip of paper) cut and stick pictures or articles on each side, making a world 'mural'. Each side of the box would represent a different continent i.e. AFRICA, AMERICAS, EUROPE, ASIA and AUSTRALASIA.

Discuss situations for prayer in each area, read letters from people you know in these areas.

People can continue to add contributions to the box each week, building up a 'global perspective'. This could involve younger people in your group.

Activity 4

Bible travellers

Using the list provided (page 127), discuss characters in the Bible who visited or moved to other countries.

Activity 5

Drama: *Jonah, the Reluctant Evangelist*, by Pat Turner.

This short sketch could be read by three people in the group with minimal preparation, or presented to a larger group using people who want to explore drama as a method of communicating the word of God. (See script on page 128)

Activity 1
World Map

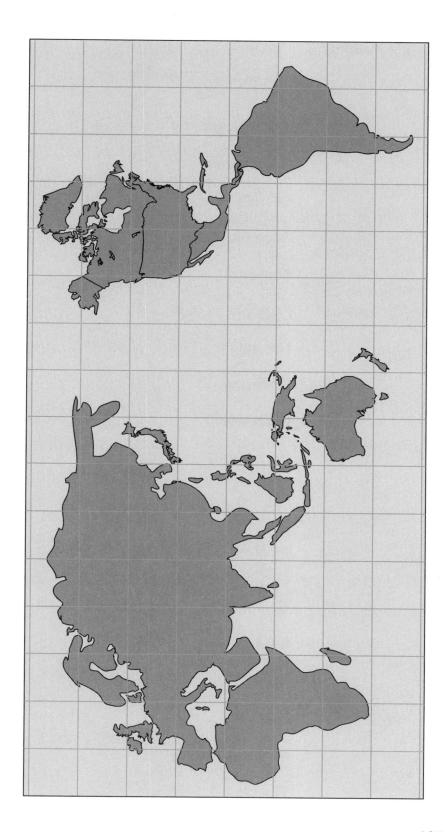

Activity 2

List of Countries/Places

BAFFIN ISLAND

BANGLADESH

BORNEO

COOK ISLANDS

ECUADOR

FALKLAND ISLANDS

FINLAND

GIBRALTAR

GUATEMALA

HONG KONG

JAMAICA

LIBYA

LITHUANIA

MAURITIUS

NEPAL

SENEGAL

SHETLAND

SRI LANKA

TASMANIA

Activity 4

Bible Travellers

CAIN	GENESIS 4:16
ABRAHAM	GENESIS 11:31, 12:1-5
ISHMAEL	GENESIS 21:9-21, 25:18
JOSEPH	GENESIS 37:1, 28
MOSES	EXOUS 2:15-25
NAOMI	RUTH 1
JONAH	JONAH 1:1-2, 3:1-6, 10
THE EXILES	2 CHRONICLES 36:11-23
QUEEN OF SHEBA	1 Kings 10:1-13
PAUL	ACTS 16:6-12

Questions

1 Where did they go to and from where?
(Use Bible atlas and a modern atlas to trace countries and routes)

2 What was the purpose of the visit or move?

3 What problems were encountered?

4 What was the immediate/short-term result?

5 What was the long-term impact of the visit/move?

Activity 5

JONAH, THE RELUCTANT EVANGELIST
Pat Turner

The cast

Jonah

Friend

Sailor

Props

Clipboard

J Hi John!

(Jonah enters in a depressingly desperate panic. The friend is an enthusiastic, gifted evangelist)

Friend What's the matter then, Jonah, old pal, old chum?

Jonah I've got a message from the boss.

Friend Oh yes. I hear he's got good things in store for you.

Jonah *(Depressed)* I don't think so. I've been sent on a mission.

Friend *(Enthusiastic. He can't help but preach!)* Entrusted, envisioned, filled with power and purpose, eager to see the Kingdom of God established in our day! . . .

Jonah . . . Yeah . . .

Friend I LOVE IT!! Evangelism – my favourite topic. I could talk for hours.

Jonah I know.

Friend Seeing changed lives . . . There's nothing like it.

Jonah That's true, but . . .

Friend Watching whole crowds responding. That's incredible! Preaching to hundreds of people makes you feel . . .

Jonah Terrified!

Friend TOTALLY EXHILARATED!

Jonah That's all right for you . . . but when I talk, nobody listens!

Friend *(Not listening)* Makes you feel fabulous.

Jonah *(Sees he was ignored. Pause)* Makes you feel a failure.

Friend Did you say something?

Jonah I'm going to fail. I can't do it! Look at me! I'm not a speaker. I'm not a preacher. I'm not a great personality . . .

Friend *(Looks at him)* No!

Jonah I can't even talk to my neighbour, never mind a city.

Friend A city?

Jonah *(Panicking)* NINEVEH! I've been sent to Nineveh! It can't be right.

Friend *(Knowing smile)* Nineveh, eh . . . Where all the men are . . . *(he grunts and mimes strong men showing off their muscles)* . . . and the girls are *(he demonstrates the curves and is enjoying it)* and the pubs *(behaves drunk)* and the clubs *(disco dances)* and the gambling and fighting *(boxes his way over to Jonah. Ends up threatening him with a punch. Jonah shrinks down)*

Jonah Yes.

Friend A CHALLENGE! I love a challenge.

Jonah I'd love a nice quiet job in a nice quiet town with a nice long lie-in on Saturdays. There's something wrong, I tell you . . . Look! . . . Just double check for me, will you?

Friend Oh, if you insist. *(Takes clipboard. Reads)*
Job description. Just tick the boxes.

(Reads the list to Jonah and marks his answers on the page)

Self confident . . .

Jonah No.

Friend Experienced speaker.

Jonah No.

Friend Star quality. *(Looks at him. Pause)*

Both No!

Friend In short, you are just not capable.

Jonah No!

Friend *(Excited)* Congratulations! Four crosses! The job's yours!

Jonah But I've got no chance!

Friend God loves a challenge.

Jonah It smells fishy to me.

Friend Don't worry about it. *(Places comforting arm around shoulder)* I'm sure you'll have a whale of a time!

(The friend leaves Jonah to panic alone. As he thinks, Jonah becomes more and more worked up)

Jonah Nineveh . . . Where the men are all *(shows muscle but is afraid of them)* . . . and the women are all *(shows curves but can't take the pressure. Wipes his forehead and loosens his collar)*

Sailor *(Offstage)* ALL ABOARD! ALL ABOARD!

Jonah *(Calls)* Does this boat go to Nineveh?

Sailor No.

Jonah *(Looks to audience for a split second)* I'll take it!

(Leaves hurriedly)

Worship Session 15

THEME: GLOBAL PERSPECTIVE

Opening words

Leader May God be gracious to us and bless us
and make his face shine upon us;
may your ways be known on earth,
your salvation among all nations.

Group *Our God reigns!*

Leader May the nations be glad and sing for joy,
for you rule the people justly and guide the nations of
the earth.

Group *Our God reigns!*

Leader Then the land will yield its harvest
and our God will bless us.
God will bless us
and all the ends of the earth will fear him.

Group *Our God reigns!*
(Adapted from Psalm 67)

Leader Jesus said, 'Go into all the world
and preach the good news to all creation.'
(Mark 16: 15)

Group *Our God reigns!*

Worship song

We want to see Jesus lifted high
Doug Horley

We want to see Jesus lifted high,
a banner that flies across this land,
that all men might see the truth
and know he is the way to heaven.
We want to see Jesus lifted high,
a banner that flies across this land,
that all men might see the truth,
and know he is the way to heaven.

We want to see, we want to see,
we want to see Jesus lifted high.
We want to see, we want to see,
we want to see Jesus lifted high.

Step by step we're moving forward,
little by little taking ground,
every prayer a powerful weapon,
strongholds come tumbling down,
and down, and down, and down.

We're gonna see . . .

© 1993 Kingsway's Thankyou Music

Reading from Scripture

Leader   Sing joyfully to the Lord, you righteous;
it is fitting for the upright to praise him.

Group   *The word of the Lord is right and true;*
he is faithful in all he does.

Leader   The Lord loves righteousness and justice;
the earth is full of his unfailing love.

Group   *Let the earth fear the Lord;*
let all the people of the world revere him.

Leader   For he spoke and it came to be;
he commanded and it stood firm.
The Lord foils the plans of the nations;
he thwarts the purposes of the peoples.

Group   *But the plans of the Lord stand firm for ever,*
the purposes of his heart through all generations.

Leader   Blessed is the nation whose God is the Lord,
the people he chose for his inheritance.
From heaven the Lord looks and sees all mankind.

Group   *From his dwelling place he watches*
all who live on the earth.

Leader   He forms the hearts of all
and considers everything they do.

Group   *No king is saved by the size of his army.*

Leader   No warrior escapes by his great strength.

Group *A horse is a vain hope for deliverance;*
despite all its great strength it cannot save.

Leader But the eyes of the Lord are on those who fear him,
on those whose hope is in his unfailing love,
to deliver them from death
and keep them alive in famine.

(Adapted from Psalm 33)

Group *Everyone who trusts in Jesus will never be put to shame.*
The Lord is Lord of all and richly blesses all who call on
him.

Leader Yes, everyone who calls on the name of the Lord
will be saved.
How then can they call on one they have not believed in?
How can they believe in one of whom they
have not heard?
How can they hear without someone preaching to them?

(From Romans 10:11-14)

Meditation and prayer

In our meditation today we are going to think about
people in all the different parts of the world, using the
globe/map as a focus.

To close

Leader From heaven the Lord looks down and sees all
mankind. From his dwelling place he watches all who
live on the earth.

Prayer and praise

Let's pray for all the people living and working for the Gospel today, in countries all over the world, and specifically for those we know.

Worship songs

We shall stand
Graham Kendrick

We shall stand
with our feet on the Rock.
Whatever they may say,
we'll lift your name up high.
And we shall walk
through the darkest night;
setting our faces like flint,
we'll walk into the light.

Lord, you have chosen me
for fruitfulness,
to be transformed
into your likeness.
I'm gonna fight on through
till I see you face to face.

Lord, as your witnesses
you've appointed us.
And with your Holy Spirit
anointed us.
And so I'll fight on through
till I see you face to face.

**Lord, have mercy
(Prayer song)**
Graham Kendrick

Lord, have mercy on us,

come and heal our land.

Cleanse with your fire,

heal with your touch.

Humbly we bow

and call upon you now.

O Lord, have mercy on us,

O Lord, have mercy on us.

© 1991 Make Way Music

Further activities

The emphasis in this session is on developing a global perspective by looking at a variety of issues including other religious viewpoints, the positive and similar aspects of world religions, and the group's fears or suspicions, ignorance or misconceptions.

Closing words

Leader From heaven the Lord looks down and sees all mankind. From his dwelling place he watches all who live on the earth.

Group *Let the earth fear the Lord;*
let all the people of the world revere him.

We want to see Jesus lifted high

Words and Music: Doug Horley

Lively

We want to see Je - sus lift - ed high,

a ban - ner that flies a - cross this land,

that all men might see the truth and know

he is the way to hea - ven. We want to see,
(We're gon - na)

we want to see, we want to see Je - sus lift - ed high.
(we're gon - na) (we're gon - na)

We shall stand

Words and Music: Graham Kendrick

2. Lord, as your witnesses
   you've appointed us.
   And with your Holy Spirit
   anointed us.
   And so I'll fight on through
   till I see you face to face.

Lord, have mercy
Prayer song

Words and Music: Graham Kendrick

Lord, have mer-cy on us, come and heal our land. Cleanse with your fire, heal with your touch. Hum-bly we bow and call up-on you now. O Lord, have mer-cy on us. O

Acknowledgements

The publishers wish to express their gratitude to the following for permission to include copyright material in this book:

Baker Book House, P.O. Box 6287, Grand Rapids, Michigan 49516-6287, USA for the extract from *Each New Day* by Corrie Ten Boom, published by Fleming H. Revell (a division of Baker Book House Co.)

CopyCare, P.O. Box 77, Hailsham, East Sussex BN27 3EF (HYPERLINK mail to: music@copycare.com) for the songs *Great is the Lord* © 1985 Body Songs; *I receive your love* © 1980 Word's Spirit of Praise Music; *Lord, I come to you* © 1992 Maranatha! Music, and *I believe in Jesus* © 1987 Mercy/Vineyard Publishing.

Hodder and Stoughton Ltd, 338 Euston Road, London NW1 3BH for the extracts from The New International Version of the Bible, © 1973, 1978, 1984 International Bible Society. All rights reserved. (NIV is a registered trademark of International Bible Society. UK trademark number 1448790) Also for the extract from *One in the Spirit* by David Watson, Hodder and Stoughton 1973.

Kingsway's Thankyou Music, P.O. Box 75, Eastbourne, East Sussex BN23 6NW, UK for the songs *You make your face to shine* © 1996 Darlene Zschech & Russell Fragar/Hillsong Music Australia; *Over the mountains* © 1994 Curious? Music; *You make my heart feel glad* © 1990 Kingsway's Thankyou Music; *From the ends of the earth* © 1996 Integrity's Hosannah! Music (UK only), and *We want to see Jesus lifted high* © 1993 Kingsway's Thankyou Music.

Make Way Music, P.O. Box 263, Croydon, CR9 5AP, UK for the songs *We shall stand* © 1988 and *Lord, have mercy* © 1991. International copyright secured. All rights reserved.

Riverside Christian Fellowship, 58 Rutland Road, Gedling, Nottinghamshire NG4 4JQ for the song *Big, mighty and strong*.

Sovereign Lifestyle Music Ltd, P.O. Box 356, Leighton Buzzard, Beds. LU7 8WP, UK for the song *Holy Spirit, we welcome you* © 1986.

Every effort has been made to trace the owners of copyright material and we hope that no copyright has been infringed. Pardon is sought and apology made if the contrary be the case, and a correction will be made in any reprint of this book.